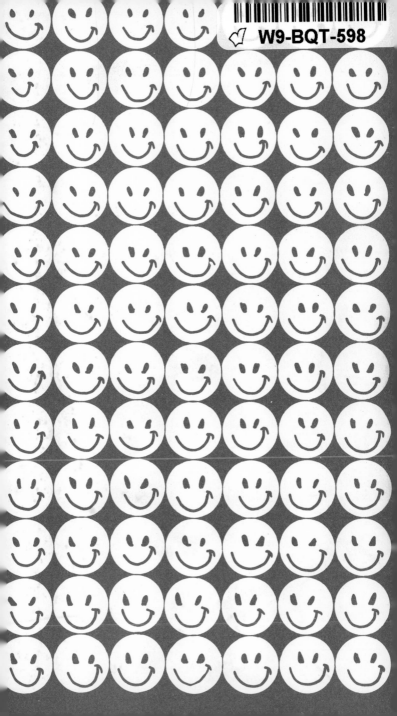

KEEP SMILING AND HAVE A HAPPY DAY

KEEP SMILING AND HAVE A HAPPY DAY

Compiled by
ALLEN JAMES

STANYAN BOOKS   RANDOM HOUSE

A Stanyan Book
Published by Stanyan Books,
8721 Sunset Blvd., Suite C
Hollywood, California 90069
and by Random House, Inc.
201 East 50th Street
New York, N.Y. 10022

Library of Congress Catalog
Card Number: 72-81615

ISBN: 0-394-48217-4

Printed in U.S.A.

Designed by Hy Fujita

The best way to cheer yourself up
is to try to cheer somebody else.

— MARK TWAIN

What sunshine is to flowers, smiles are to humanity. They are but trifles, to be sure, but scattered along life's pathway, the good they do is inconceivable.

— **Joseph Addison**

What's the use of worrying?
It never was worthwhile,
So, pack up your troubles in
     your old kit-bag,
And smile, smile, smile.

          — GEORGE ASAF
            Pack Up Your Troubles in
            Your Old Kit-Bag

Smiling is one of the best relaxation
exercises I know of.

               — HENRY MILLER

Man is distinguished from all other
creatures by the faculty of laughter.

— **JOSEPH ADDISON**

Humor is laughing at what you haven't
got when you ought to have it.

— **LANGSTON HUGHES**

There's a town called
Don't-You-Worry
On the banks of the
River Smile
Where the Cheer-up
and Be-happy
Blossom sweetly all
the while.

— I. J. Bartlett

It is a sort of survival quality that came down with us through the ages that we must take adversity with a smile or a joke.

— **STEPHEN LEACOCK**

Someone once defined humor as a way to keep from killing yourself.

— **ABE BURROWS**

People are much too solemn —
I'm all for sticking pins into
episcopal behinds.

— ALDOUS HUXLEY

If you don't learn to laugh at trouble,
you won't have anything to laugh at
when you're old.

— ED HOWE

With the fearful
strain that is on me
night and day, if I
did not laugh I
should die.

— Abraham Lincoln

Any man who has
had the job I've had
and didn't have a
sense of humor
wouldn't still
be here.

— Harry S. Truman

Every time a man smiles—but much more so when he laughs— it adds something to this fragment of life.

— **Laurence Sterne**

Mirth is God's medicine.

— **HENRY WARD BEECHER**

Be of good cheer:
this counsel is of Heaven.

— **HOMER**
Odyssey

A light heart lives long.

— **WILLIAM SHAKESPEARE**
Love's Labor's Lost

A little levity will save many a good
heavy thing from sinking.

— **SAMUEL BUTLER**

That's a joke, son!

— "SENATOR CLAGHORN"
The Fred Allen Show

As she is going to be married next
month, she is busy getting her
torso ready.

— BESSIE LORRAINE BOLES

The parting injunctions
   Of mothers and wives
Are one of those functions
   That poison their lives.

— CLARENCE DAY

Lines to three boys,
3, 6½, and 2 years of age:
Gentlemen, I love you and like you
Caring little for your IQ.

— FRANKLIN P. ADAMS

He must not laugh at his own wheeze:
A snuff box has no right to sneeze.

— KEITH PRESTON

Child of the pure,
     unclouded brown
And dreaming eyes
     of wonder!
Though time be fleet
     and I and thou
Are half a life asunder,
Thy loving smile will
     surely hail
The love-gift of a
     fairy tale.

— Lewis Carroll
   Introduction to *Through The
   Looking Glass*

Oh, don't you remem-
  ber sweet Alice,
  Ben Bolt?
Sweet Alice, whose
  hair was so brown,
Who wept with delight
  when you gave
  her a smile,
And trembled with fear
  at your frown?

— **Thomas Dunn English**
Ben Bolt

The most thoroughly wasted of all days
is that on which one has not laughed.

— **NICOLAS CHAMFORT**

You grow up the day you have the
first real laugh — at yourself.

— **ETHEL BARRYMORE**

Even Olympus needed the corrective
of laughter. When they kicked
Momus out, the deities degenerated
into sots and jades.

— **DON MARQUIS**

The capacity for laughter has never
been granted to man before the
fortieth day from his birth, and then
it is looked upon as a miracle
of precocity.

— **PLINY THE ELDER**

Let care kill a cat.
We'll laugh and grow fat.

— **ANONYMOUS**

The smile that flickers on baby's lips when he sleeps—does anybody know where it was born? Yes, there is a rumor that a young pale beam of a crescent moon touched the edge of a vanishing autumn cloud, and there the smile was first born in the dream of a dew-washed morning.

— **Rabindranath Tagore**

In came Mrs. Fezziwig, one vast substantial smile.

— **Charles Dickens**
A *Christmas Carol*

When Irish Eyes Are Smiling

Smile, Darn You, Smile

When You're Smiling

Smile For Me

A Smile Will Go a Long, Long Way

Let a Smile Be Your Umbrella

Smile—You're On Candid Camera

Smile and the world smiles with you.
— **SAYING**

Smiles Of a Summer Night
— **FILM TITLE**

Watch the birdie. Smile!
— **LAUGH-IN
TV SHOW**

Keep Smiling and Have a Happy Day
— **BOOK TITLE**

It seems there were these three rabbits who lived together. One was named Foot, the second one Foot Foot, and the third was called Foot Foot Foot.

One day Foot was feeling quite badly, so Foot Foot and Foot Foot Foot took Foot to a doctor. After examining Foot, the doctor spoke to Foot Foot and Foot Foot Foot. "I'm afraid there isn't much I can do for your friend," he said. "He's very sick."

Sure enough, after only a week, Foot died, and Foot Foot and Foot Foot Foot were distraught. Then one morning the following month Foot Foot said to Foot Foot Foot, "I feel terrible." So Foot Foot Foot packed up Foot Foot and took him off to another doctor. "We'll get a good doctor this time," Foot Foot Foot said to Foot Foot. "That last one certainly didn't help Foot."

The new doctor gave Foot Foot a thorough physical examination and reported to Foot Foot Foot that Foot Foot was very ill indeed. Foot Foot Foot became hysterical. "You've just *got* to save him doctor! We already have one Foot in the grave."

Although the great professional comics have generally been men, like Chaplin and Fernandel, they must be thought of as exceptions to their sex. The average man very rarely has the comic touch; but in women it is almost universal, though they often keep it under wraps.

— **Jack Smith**
Los Angeles Times

Humor is merely tragedy standing
on its head with its pants torn.

— IRVIN S. COBB

Humor is emotional chaos
remembered in tranquility.

— JAMES THURBER

It is a particular quirk
of American character
that you can call an
American almost any
name you like and you
will get either a mild
rebuttal or some prot-
estation. But if you tell
somebody he has no
sense of humor, he's
really going to hit you
in the mouth.

— Hal Kanter

Men will confess to treason, murder, arson, false teeth or a wig. How many of them will own up to a lack of humor?

— FRANK M. COLBY

Any man will admit, if need be, that his sight is not good, or that he cannot swim, or shoots badly with a rifle, but to touch upon his sense of humor is to give him a mortal affront.

— STEPHEN LEACOCK

The human race has only one really
effective weapon, and that is laughter.

— **MARK TWAIN**

And unextinguished laughter
shakes the skies.

— **HOMER**
Iliad

A good laugh is sunshine in a house.

— **WILLIAM M. THACKERAY**

We're all here for a spell;
get all the good laughs you can.

— **WILL ROGERS**

The silvery fabric of a laugh.

— **R. H. NEWELL**

Laughter makes good blood.

— **ITALIAN SAYING**

A maid that laughs is half taken.

— **JOHN RAY**

A man isn't poor if he can still laugh.

— **RAYMOND HITCHCOCK**

We are growing serious, and let me
tell you, that's the very next step
to being dull.

— **JOSEPH ADDISON**

Man alone suffers so excruciatingly
in the world that he was compelled
to invent laughter.

— **NIETZSCHE**

A man without mirth is like a wagon without springs—he is jolted by every pebble in the road.

— HENRY WARD BEECHER

Smiling through tears.

— HOMER

There is no defense against adverse fortune which is so effectual as an habitual sense of humor.

— THOMAS HIGGINSON

39

A ghoulish old fellow
   in Kent
Encrusted his wife in
   cement;
He said, with a sneer,
"I was careful, my
   dear,
To follow your natural
   bent."

— Morris Bishop

Billy, in one of his nice
    new sashes,
Fell in the fire and was
    burnt to ashes;
Now, although the
    room grows chilly,
I haven't the heart to
    poke poor Billy.
— **Harry Graham**

Then I commended mirth,
because a man hath no better
thing under the sun than to eat,
and to drink, and to be merry.

— ECCLESIASTES, 8

A life without humor is like a life without
legs. You are haunted by a sense of
incompleteness, and you cannot go
where your friends go.

— FRANK MOORE COLBY

If I'd known you were planning to seat people on both sides of me, I'd have had my nose fixed.

— **Barbra Streisand**
(*to Cocoanut Grove audience*)

But still a pun I do detest,
'Tis such a paltry humbug jest;
They who've least wit make them best.

— WILLIAM COMBE

Of puns it has been said that they
who most dislike them are least
able to utter them.

— EDGAR ALLAN POE

A pun is the lowest form of humor—
when you don't think of it first.

— OSCAR LEVANT

Gnus are used chiefly by a certain class of authors for making atrocious puns, such as "No Gnus is good Gnus," and "Happy Gnu Year!" This will go on forever, because you can't teach an old Gnu tricks.

— **Will Cuppy**

The church to which I belong is where the oftener you laugh the better, because by laughter only can you destroy evil without malice.

— Bernard Shaw

Only in this world do we laugh. In hell it won't be possible and in heaven, it won't be proper.

— **Jules Renard**

The thing that goes
   the farthest toward
   making life worth
   while
That costs the least,
   and does the most,
   is just a pleasant
   smile.

— **Wilbur D. Nesbit**

Even children followed with endearing
    wile
And plucked his gown, to share the
    good man's smile.

— OLIVER GOLDSMITH
The Deserted Village

If we do meet again, why, we
    shall smile;
If not, why then, this parting
    was well made.

— WILLIAM SHAKESPEARE
Julius Caesar

Haste thee, Nymph, and bring with thee
Jest, and youthful jollity,
Quips and cranks and wanton wiles,
Nods and becks and wreathed smiles.

— JOHN MILTON

Her loveliness I never knew
Until she smiled on me.

— HARTLEY COLERIDGE

Milton Berle for years has been bragging to audiences that he has stolen jokes from other comedians. There has been no reason to doubt his word.

— **Fred Allen**

I smile so seldom that I wonder at Arlene Francis who smiles persistently. Like the Sorcerer's Apprentice, once she turns it on, can she turn it off?

— *Oscar Levant*
Memoirs of an Amnesiac

How much lies in laughter: the cipher-key, wherewith we decipher the whole man.

— THOMAS CARLYLE

Strange, when you come to think of it, that of the countless folk who have lived before our time on this planet, not one is known in history or in legend as having died of laughter.

— MAX BEERBOHM

Laughter is the sensation of
feeling good all over, and showing
it principally in one spot.

— JOSH BILLINGS

Laughter is the bark of delight of a
gregarious animal at the proximity of
his kind . . . Laughter is the female
of tragedy . . . Laughter is the
mind sneezing.

— WYNDHAM LEWIS

Humor is falling downstairs,
if you do it in the act of warning
your wife not to.

— **KENNETH BIRD**

Humor is your own smile
surprising you in your mirror.

— **LANGSTON HUGHES**

Humor is an affirmation of dignity,
a declaration of man's superiority
to all that befalls him.

— **ROMAIN GARY**

We Irish never hesitate to give a serious thought the benefit and halo of a laugh.

— Sean O'Casey

Do you smile because you are happy?
Put it the other way round—smile,
and you're immediately happy.

— BEVINS JAY

Care to our coffin adds a nail,
   no doubt,
And every grin so merry
   draws one out.

— JOHN WOLCOT

Humor issues not in laughter,
but in still smiles, which lie
far deeper.
— THOMAS CARLYLE

True humor springs not more from
the head than from the heart.
It is not contempt; its
essence is love.
— THOMAS CARLYLE

The man that loves and laughs
must sure do well.
— ALEXANDER POPE

I think funny.

— **ABE BURROWS**

Anything awful makes me laugh.
I once misbehaved at a funeral.

— **CHARLES LAMB**

Good taste and humor are a
contradiction in terms,
like a chaste whore.

— MALCOLM MUGGERIDGE

The world likes humor, but treats it
patronizingly. It decorates its serious
artists with laurel, and its wags
with Brussels sprouts.

— E. B. WHITE

Sweet Peace is crowned with smiles.

— HENRY VAUGHAN

Where the quiet-colored end
of evening smiles.

— ROBERT BROWNING

Reproof on her lip, but a smile
in her eye.

— SAMUEL LOVER

Better by far you should forget
    and smile
Than that you should remember
    and be sad.

— CHRISTINA ROSSETTI

As happy a man
as any in the world,
for the whole
world seems to smile
upon me.

— **Samuel Pepys**